Original title:
Tropical Heatwaves

Copyright © 2025 Creative Arts Management OÜ
All rights reserved.

Author: Julian Montgomery
ISBN HARDBACK: 978-1-80581-569-3
ISBN PAPERBACK: 978-1-80581-096-4
ISBN EBOOK: 978-1-80581-569-3

A Cove of Pulsing Heat

In the cove where sweat does flow,
The sun beats down, oh what a show!
I fry an egg upon the sand,
As locals laugh, it's quite unplanned.

Beach balls bounce, they soar and sway,
But watch your drink, it warms away!
The ice cubes dance, begin to melt,
A sunburn's gift is soon be-felt.

Flip-flops stick, they make a sound,
As happy folks jump all around!
With sunscreen smeared from head to toe,
They grumble loud, "Oh, where'd the shade go?"

Lemons squeezed in drinks, oh taste!
A cloudy drink, we never waste!
The breeze is scarce, the laughter grand,
As sandcastles sink like dreams unplanned.

Drenched Dreams at Dusk

Sun sets low, the sweat begins,
Bikini lines and mismatched fins.
Ice cream melts, oh what a mess,
Sipping lemonade with sunburned chest.

Flip-flops squish in sandy bays,
Sidewalks shimmer in lazy rays.
We dance with laughter in balmy air,
As seagulls steal our snacks with flair.

Whirlwind of Warmth

The breeze is bold, it fluffs my hair,
A sunburned nose, I do not care.
Sunscreen wars, we battle for fun,
Invisible foes before we run.

Hats fly off in the gusty swirl,
Boys shout 'catch!' in a dizzy twirl.
Sandcastles melt in the afternoon glow,
As the ice cream truck plays tunes we know.

The Euphoria of Elation

Bright beach balls bounce from kid to kid,
Adults sip drinks with a silly skid.
Barbecue smoke rises like dreams,
While seagulls compete with raucous screams.

Sunshine laughs, we join in cheer,
Every splash brings us near.
Oh, what joy in the sweetness of play,
Worries dissolve with the heat of the day.

Ignition of the Skies

Fireflies flicker as darkness grows,
Sun-kissed skin feels the night's cool flows.
With every giggle, the stars ignite,
Silly shadows dance, oh what a sight!

Chasing dusk with our goofy glee,
Laughter ripples like waves at sea.
Under the warm sky's twinkling spree,
It's fun forever, just you and me.

Reverie in the Sidewalk Heat.

Sweat beads rolling down my brow,
I swear I saw a mirage now.
A hot dog cart just turned to gold,
Or was it me, too hot to hold?

Flip-flops melting to the street,
I dance like I lost my feet.
Neighbors peek from shaded shade,
While ice cream drips and kids parade.

Sun-Soaked Reverie

A sunburned lobster, that's my fate,
With SPF dreams that came too late.
Sipping lemonade with extra ice,
While ants perform their salsa slice.

The grass sizzles, a crunchy treat,
Bare toes roasting in the heat.
The dog looks like a furry fry,
As we both question how to fly.

Mirage of the Sun

There's a pool that shimmers in the haze,
But it turns out, it's just a phase.
I dive into a fountain's mist,
But land in bubbles, I can't resist.

A sun hat floats like a stylish boat,
While clouds play hide and seek, I gloat.
Tanned and grilled like summer meat,
I laugh and sing, 'Aloha, heat!'

Searing Sands at Dusk

The sand's a blanket, hot as toast,
As crabs march by, we laugh the most.
Counting calories from chips we eat,
While the seagulls plan their high-stakes feat.

With jellyfish balloons floating near,
I chase them down without a fear.
Dusk arrives, the sun takes a bow,
Tomorrow's fun, I'll make a vow.

Batter of the Wavy Seas

The sun drops down like buttered toast,
Seagulls squawk, they're yelling, "Coast!"
My ice cream drips like it's in a race,
On the sand, it's a slippery place.

Flip-flops squish, what a classic sound,
As I chase my hat that's blown around.
A crab waves hi, or is it a dance?
I'll join in, let's give it a chance!

Hidden in the Golden Glow

In shorts so bright they could blind a bee,
I lounge so hard, my drink's on me.
The beach ball's lost in a neighboring yard,
Looks like my game's about to be hard.

Around me, sunscreen flies like confetti,
My friend just slipped; oh, wasn't that steady?
We'll tan so much, we'll look like toast,
But laughter's the best; it's what we boast!

The Poem in the Aftersun

Noon's heat wraps me like a warm blanket,
With each sip of soda, I shall not prank it.
A sandcastle rises with a sloppy grin,
While my toes are buried, let the fun begin!

Naps are a must under this sticky sky,
But watch out for crabs; they sneakily pry.
A seagull squawks in dramatic flair,
I'll trade him a fry for some beach-side air!

Painted Skies of Desire

The sunset colors splash like paint on a wall,
With hues so bright, I'm caught in their thrall.
My friend yells, "Look! A dolphin or two!"
Turns out it's just a dude in a canoe!

A sunset selfie, we pose with a grin,
But in the frame, there's an unexpected fin!
The ocean's antics always steal the show,
With laughter and smiles, we dance and we glow!

Golden Horizon's Embrace

The sun's a giant lemon drop,
Squeezing juice on all we wear.
Flip-flops dance on sizzling sand,
While ice cream drips without a care.

Surfers ride the molten waves,
Surfboards melting in the sun.
Seagulls squawk with sunburned wings,
As beach days morph to sticky fun.

Hats fly off like kites in breeze,
Chasing shade beneath a palm.
Sweaty smiles and laughter tease,
Underneath that golden calm.

The Hum of Warmth

The air hums like a lazy bee,
Dancing round our sticky skin.
Lemonade spills and giggles flee,
As sunburns start to creep in.

Bikinis cling like second skin,
We swim like fish in tar.
Each splash a little laugh and grin,
While sunscreen's lost—oh, bizarre!

Fans are spinning, drinks are cold,
But sweat drops still make their track.
We joke 'bout heat, the fiery hold,
And who's first to take a snack.

Fever Dream of the Land

Oven mitts on sizzling sun,
We roast and toast—who's next to fry?
Dance like chicken, have some fun,
While shades of heatwave make us sigh.

Blow on drinks, like magic wands,
Each sip's a tiny, frosty treat.
Salty chips and messy hands,
This sun can't be beat!

Neighbors brag of tan lines scored,
While melting popsicles drip low.
In sticky thrills, we won't be bored,
Savoring summer's bright glow.

Oasis of Hopes

A mirage blooms with every wave,
Mocking thirst like playful friends.
We chase the coolness that we crave,
In laughter where the summer bends.

Frogs wear flip-flops, crabs tap dance,
Sprinklers spray in sun's embrace.
Splashing water's sweet romance,
In this swamp of palm and grace.

Dreaming of a frosty place,
As we guzzle coconut cream.
Underneath this sunlit face,
Every moment's one big dream.

Sunkissed Shadows on Sandy Shores

The sun is a giant frying pan,
Bacon sizzles in the sand.
Umbrellas are flapping like flags,
While crabs hitch a ride on a hand.

Sunglasses sliding down the nose,
Even seagulls are sweating too.
Flip-flops dance off by themselves,
While beach balls play peek-a-boo.

Ice cream drips faster than the sun,
Sticky hands multiply in size.
Laughter mixes with salty seas,
As we try to keep our fries.

And when the heat gets really wild,
We dive into the ocean's brew.
Only to find it's a warm bath,
With fish that laugh at me and you.

Embrace of the Sweltering Day

The pavement's hot enough to fry,
An egg without a pan nearby.
People waddle like lost penguins,
Seeking shade, oh my, oh my!

Sweaty shirts cling like best friends,
While popsicles melt and drip.
A sprinkler's dance becomes our joy,
As we dive and execute a flip.

Fans are whirring, blowing hot air,
While kids are racing 'round the square.
With each splash, we shout and squeal,
A summer dream, surreal appeal.

And when the sun bids us goodnight,
Fireflies twinkle, oh what a sight!
But tomorrow, the cycle resumes,
As we waltz with heat and fun resumes!

Coral Reefs in Golden Light

Underwater beauty shines so bright,
With fish dancing in carefree flight.
The coral laughs with colors bold,
While sunbeams make the ocean gold.

Snorkels bobbing like wild ducks,
As we take on the sea's quick plucks.
Lost in bubbles and salty waves,
Pretending we're the ocean's knaves.

A lobster's grin as wide as the day,
While turtles glide, leading the way.
We wiggle like jelly, get stuck in weeds,
And chase the charm of underwater deeds.

Emerging from the splashes, we cheer,
"Isn't this the finest time of year?"
While gulls above squawk lofty dreams,
And bubbles burst with giggly screams.

Lush Eden Beneath a Blazing Sky

In gardens where the flowers toast,
And lizards flaunt a lazy boast.
Sweating under a sweet sunbeam,
We sip cold drinks and laugh, it seems.

Coconut palms sway like dancers,
In a heat that prompts wild prancers.
Bees buzz like they're in a race,
While squirrels hide in leafy space.

Picnics turn into sticky affairs,
As ants join our snacks with bold flares.
We trade stories under shady trees,
A chorus of laughter and buzzing bees.

As twilight approaches with no retreat,
The temperature drops, but not our beat.
With smiles wide as the stars appear,
We dance to the rhythm of summer here.

The Last Light of an Endless Day

The sun drips slow, like melted ice,
Flip-flops squeak, they roll like dice.
A parrot squawks in a cheeky tone,
While beach balls make a break for home.

The blender roars with a fruity song,
Sipping cocktails, it feels so wrong.
A crab scuttles by, in a hurry indeed,
Turns back to stare, like it's on a deed.

With skin that glistens like fresh-cut fruit,
Watch out for sandals, they're off, to boot!
The sunset laughs, as day turns to night,
And shadows get tangled in the fading light.

Driftwood Stories in the Glow

On driftwood couches, we share our tales,
With sun-bleached laughter and strange emails.
A seashell whispers secrets so sweet,
While sand dances up in a funky beat.

Flip the pages of seaweed dreams,
As dolphins plot their shiny schemes.
A coconut falls, oh what a surprise,
Cracking us up, our laughter will rise.

Beneath the stars, we trade silly grins,
Fishing for giggles, where no one wins.
Caught in the glow of a campfire's cheer,
Every shenanigan brought us all near.

Sunlit Etiquettes of Laughter

Sunscreen's a must, but who puts it on?
We giggle and squirm until it's gone.
The UV rays set our plans in motion,
While beach umbrellas sway like the ocean.

Salty snacks on a sliding scale,
One chip too many? Let's follow the trail!
Watermelon fights are in full play,
Juice dripping down in a silly display.

We dance on sand, with feet all a-jive,
Summoning joy just to feel alive.
With every wave crashing in on cue,
The tide reminds us, laughter feels new.

The Colors of a Blazing Twilight

As dusk arrives with a vibrant rush,
The skies explode in a technicolor crush.
We dip and twirl without a care,
While flamingos pose with a fashion flare.

The grill smokes up with a spicy tease,
Strangers unite, now friends with ease.
Burgers flip as laughter roars,
A chef with style, who plays to applause.

Fishes leap like they're in a race,
Making leaps that would put us to disgrace.
Joy bursts forth in this fading light,
Each moment bright, until stars take flight.

When the Earth Sizzles

The sun's a giant frying pan,
Making me feel like a crispy man.
Sweat's dripping down like a leaky tap,
I think I'll just lay down on a mat.

Ice cream's melting faster than a wink,
Sticky fingers make me start to rethink.
Coconut water's my new best friend,
We laugh and giggle, this heat won't end.

Mirages dance on the scorching street,
Sandals complain, with every little beat.
A squirrel dives in a splashy pool,
While I sit here, feeling like a fool.

The sun waves bye as I sip my drink,
Cheers to the warmth, as I start to sink.
When life's a sauna, embrace the fun,
Bring on the laughter, let's soak in the sun!

Secrets Beneath the Palm Leaves

Underneath the palms, the secrets sway,
A coconut thinks it can sway all day.
Lizards wear shades to chill and prance,
While I'm drenched in sweat, what a wild dance!

The pineapples giggle, they're feeling fine,
Winking at melons, say, 'Try the brine!'
Insects throw parties with their tiny wings,
While I'm here daydreaming of cooler things.

I tried to grill hot dogs in the sun,
But they cooked too fast, and now they run!
I chase them in circles, it's all a mess,
Who knew that heat could cause such distress?

So I sit in the shade, sipping my drink,
While the squirrels play games and chickens clink.
The secrets they share are juicy and sweet,
In this sunlit world, there's no such defeat!

The Lure of Lysosomes

In the heat, cells dance, oh what a sight,
Lysosomes jiving, feeling just right.
They munch on leftovers, like it's a feast,
Cleaning up after the smash of a beast.

I tried to join them in cellular fun,
But I tripped on my feet and fell with a thud.
The ribosomes chuckled, 'What's up with you?'
I rolled in the heat, like a heated stew.

DNA's hiding, it's still in a twist,
Preparing for summer—oh, what a list!
Proteins are sunbathing, looking sleek,
While I'm just here, sweating non-stop for a week.

So let's laugh at science, embrace all the heat,
Making biology feel like a comedic treat.
In this cell party under the sun,
Who would have thought that heat could be fun?

Heatborne Echoes

The echoes bounce off the steamy ground,
Whispers of warmth wrap all around.
Cats are stretched out in the golden rays,
Planning their naps for the longest of days.

A parrot complains about too much sun,
While I swap my shirt, it's too much fun.
The watermelon gang's having a blast,
Rolling around, wishing this heat would last.

My ice cubes are having a pool party race,
While I'm desperately seeking shade's embrace.
The air is thick with giggles and cheer,
What's that they say? 'Summer's finally here!'

So here's to the echoes of laughter and play,
In this world where the sun shares its sway.
Embrace the warmth, let it tickle your toes,
For life's a party, where the sweet summer flows!

The Breath of Sultry Evenings

The sun melts on the pavement's face,
As I try to find a shaded space.
My ice cream is a puddle now,
Oh, summer, how you take your bow!

The cat sprawls out in lazy ways,
Too hot for any feline plays.
Even the birds sweat while they sing,
Complaining 'bout that sticky fling!

A barbecue awaits the sun's retreat,
But the heat makes my burgers beat.
They sizzle, crackle, then just lie,
What a gift; a feathery fry!

So let's dance in this spicy air,
With glasses raised, a daring flair.
Laughing as we feign a sprint,
'Til the sweat says we need a hint!

Sunlit Dreams and Allure

The rays beam down like playful darts,
My flip-flops sing their summer parts.
Each step a squish, a sticky sound,
My toes have practically drowned!

With lemonade and sunburn's blush,
We search for shade in a frantic rush.
The sun's a jester with his tricks,
Tanning pools, but turns to bricks!

Sandcastles lean, then tumble down,
As I reign queen without a crown.
The wind laughs, tosses hair askew,
Who needs a mirror? I'm a zoo!

As evening comes, the sweat congeals,
But laughter's warmth is what heals.
We'll toast to this heat, our good friend,
Until autumn says it's time to mend.

Figments in the Heat

A mirage dances on the street,
Is that a unicorn or just the heat?
My mind's a stew, bubbling over,
Chasing ghosts of sodas and clover.

Sweat beads trickle like a race,
Mocking my slow-motion pace.
I swear that puddle winked at me,
Creepy jests of a playful spree!

My barbecue skills go up in smoke,
As I don't realize it's a joke.
Charred on the outside, raw within,
Dinner's served, let the fun begin!

The stars come out for a dreamy sigh,
While the night whispers, "give it a try."
So dance like no one sees your sweat,
This heat's a figment, I won't forget!

Essence of the Spiced Breeze

A breeze comes through, yet it's a tease,
It stirs my drink but brings no ease.
My hat flies off with a woosh and twirl,
The wind laughs hard; it gives a whirl!

The scent of BBQ, a siren's call,
Yet the sweat drips down like a waterfall.
I reach for chips, but they stick to my hand,
Snack-time decision? It's really quite bland!

The ice cream truck pulls up with glee,
But the line's like waiting for a decree.
I ponder flavors, all seem divine,
'Til I see a seagull eye my swine!

At night when the stars start to gleam,
I'll sip my drink and start to dream.
But now, in this daze of balmy fun,
I'll just embrace the quirk of sun!

Flickering Flames of Dusk

The sidewalk sizzles beneath my feet,
As sweat pools like lemonade, oh so sweet.
The sun winks down with a fiery glare,
And palm trees dance like they just don't care.

I try to sip my drink, but it spills,
Like a fountain of joy, my laughter thrills.
The ice cubes melt in a jittery game,
While the breeze whispers softly, calling my name.

My flip-flops squeak with each jolly stride,
As lizards sunbathe, adorned with pride.
The frosty treats melt faster than light,
Oh, why did I think it was a good bite?

With laughter echoing through the balmy night,
I juggle my snacks in a comical fight.
It's a circus of fun with the stars above,
In this heat, oh yes, I've found my love.

Kisses from the Sun

Sunbeams tickle the back of my neck,
I wave to the shadow, what the heck?
The beach is a dance floor, come join my show,
As seagulls caw, 'What a bummer to know!'

My melting ice cream resembles a pool,
But treat it like art—let it be cool.
The barista smiles, but I'm so bereft,
'Can I get just one drink? I've lost the rest!'

Sunscreen squirts, a slippery plot,
I'm trying to cover all I've got.
With each little blob, I'm a sight to behold,
Like a pizza chef gone a bit bold.

A tan line appears, a brand-new design,
I strut like a model—'Oh, isn't this fine?'
But the sun bites back with its last little sting,
And I'm a lobster now, just call me King!

A Canvas of Dusk and Dawn

Morning breaks with a goofy grin,
While the coffee brews with a mischievous spin.
Dancing in shadows, I twist and twirl,
As the roosters crow—oh, what a whirl!

The midday sun plays peek-a-boo,
With flaming hats and a sky so blue.
Each drip of sweat is a badge of glee,
As I challenge the heat—'Come play with me!'

Sunsets spill colors like a painter's gleam,
With hues that sparkle like a child's dream.
The crickets sing, and the stars parade,
In the carnival of night, I'm blissfully swayed.

But wait, what's this? The fireflies dance!
With tiny lights, they lead a trance.
I join their waltz, a gleeful sight,
In this silly world, everything feels right.

Waves of Breathless Laughter

I jumped in the ocean, what a splash!
With a wave of delight, I made quite the crash.
But the tide pulls me back with a teasing grin,
'You think you can stay, well let's begin!'

Floating like a noodle in the sparkling sea,
The sun plays tricks, it's no place to be.
As seagulls chuckle and dive for a snack,
I splash and shout, 'No holding back!'

Sand castles crumble, my royal abode,
I laugh as I watch them, a comical load.
With buckets and shovels, my tools of the trade,
I'm crafting a fortress that's destined to fade.

The sun dips low, painting skies with delight,
With friends all around, we dance in the light.
The warmth wraps around like a silly old hug,
In this moment of joy, I feel so snug.

Echoes of Laughter in the Heat

Sunshine sizzles, melting my shoes,
Lizards laugh as they share their views.
Sweat drips down, like a leaky tap,
I dance with the breeze and take a nap.

Coconut drinks slip through sticky hands,
Neighbors shout as the ice cream stands.
Flip-flops slap like a clapping crowd,
Even the sun thinks it's too loud!

Parrots squawk with their comedic flair,
Mangoes roll like they haven't a care.
I trip on a flip-flop, land in the sand,
Pineapple hats? I just can't understand!

But through all the foolishness we share,
Laughter bubbles, floating in the air.
So here's to the day, let's make it bright,
In this humor sun-soaked delight!

Afternoon Gaze into the Azure Abyss

Clouds look like cotton candy flown,
As I stretch out like a lazy crone.
Waves tumble in with a goofy dance,
While crabs scuttle, they've got no chance.

Seagulls squawk, trying to steal my fries,
With beady eyes, they plot and devise.
I shield my snacks while bathing my toes,
In this game of wits, who really knows?

Parasol shade is a warzone bright,
My drink's gone warm, but it feels just right.
A thousand sunbeams are tickling my nose,
I giggle at how this chaos grows!

While friends dive deep, I just sunbathe,
To the shouts and splashes, I laugh and wave.
In this azure warmth, we fell, we play,
Like children lost in a bright ballet!

Captured in the Glow of the Sun

Sunrise kisses with whispers of gold,
As we gather around, stories unfold.
Laughter erupts like popcorn on heat,
In this bright realm, we dance on our feet.

The grill smokes like a dragon at play,
Hot dogs roll fast, hoping to stay.
Though burnt offerings might hit the fan,
We toss back giggles, that's our grand plan.

Sunscreen battles turn into a game,
With war paint slathered, you can't feel the shame.
A slip and a slide on the grass, oh dear,
We tumble and giggle, sharing pure cheer!

Captured by rays, our spirits take flight,
As we sway like palm trees, all day and night.
Here's to the fun in this blaring sun,
With laughter as golden as the day is done!

Sipping Nectar Beneath the Palms

Beneath the palms, the chatter flows,
With drinks so cold, our faces glow.
Each sip a burst of fruity delight,
We laugh at the sun, how it beams so bright.

The breeze whispers secrets, no one can hear,
As my straw dances, pulling up cheer.
Coconuts roll with a natural grace,
Chasing each other in a friendly race.

Laughter rises like bubbles in soda,
While ants plot mischief, a tiny commando.
I spill my drink, what a sticky mess!
Yet here we thrive, we couldn't care less.

So raise your glasses, let's toast the day,
In this haven, we giggle and play.
With sunshine pouring and joy so warm,
In each other's laughter, we find our charm.

The Luminescence of a Fiery Dusk

When sunsets turn the world to gold,
The sun slips off its pants, I'm told.
It dances with the palm trees high,
While we just sweat and wonder why.

A lizard in a tiny hat,
Claims he's the king of all that's fat.
He basks upon a rock so bold,
Sipping shade like it's pure gold.

And lo! The crabs with their crabby jokes,
Scuttle away from sunbaked folks.
They chuckle as we grimace and sweat,
While sipping drinks we won't forget.

A beachball rolls into a fray,
Where children scream and splashes play.
The heat's a friend to laughter's sound,
As sunburned warriors gather 'round.

Beneath the Lustrous Canopy

Beneath the trees where shadows dance,
The monkeys plot their next romance.
With stolen fruit and silly pranks,
They laugh at all our sunburned thanks.

A parrot shouts, 'Is it too hot?',
While lying on a melting spot.
Its feathers gleam like summer wine,
It seems to think it's just divine.

The breeze arrives, a playful tease,
It whirls our hats like autumn leaves.
We chase them down, it's quite a sight,
As laughter echoes with delight.

And as the sky begins to glow,
In shades of pink, the sunsets show.
We gather 'round with drinks in hand,
Feeling sticky, but oh so grand.

Grains of Time on Sun-Baked Streets

The pavement sizzles where we tread,
With flip-flops flapping, feet like lead.
A dog stares back with goofy eyes,
As if to ask, 'Why not the fries?'

Ice cream drips from cones like fate,
Melting quickly; can't be late!
As kids chase shadows, the day feels bright,
While we melt into the fading light.

Our sandy feet, a tale to tell,
Of sticky heat and sunlit spell.
With laughter shared and voices loud,
We make our mark, a crazy crowd.

As crickets chirp their evening tune,
We toast the sun, the silly moon.
With cups held high, we cheer and yell,
For memories forged in heat's warm spell.

Of Hibiscus Blooms and Amber Skies

In gardens where bright blossoms beam,
The bees are buzzing, living the dream.
Hibiscus blushes like our cheeks,
While neighbors whisper funny peaks.

A chameleon, oh what a sight,
Changes colors in playful plight.
It laughs at us, we sweat and stew,
While it settles for the perfect hue.

Amber skies at dusk bring cheer,
As mosquitoes join the buzzing sphere.
We swat and stumble, dance in a line,
Embracing the madness, oh how divine.

Underneath the starry misty light,
We share tales of the day's delights.
With belly laughs and stories spun,
Tropical fun, our day is done.

Sun-Kissed Journeys

In the sun, my ice cream melts,
A sticky treat, oh how it pelts!
I chase the shade, my friend will mock,
"You're running slow, like a clock on rock!"

Flip-flops flapping, what a sound,
As I dodge the heat, I jump around.
Sipping drinks, so icy cold,
My brain is fried, but my heart is bold!

Sweaty brow, a shimmering sheen,
I dance like I'm in a sauna scene.
Sunscreen wars, who needs the tan?
With a ghostly glow, I'm a beachy man!

So here's to trips where we all sweat,
In nature's oven, we have no regret.
With each hot step, our laughter flies,
Under the sun, we find our highs!

Mirage Musings

A distant palm, what's that I see?
Is it a mirage or just a tree?
The heat waves dance, the air's a blur,
I swear my drink just made a purr!

Sunburnt noses, we look quite bright,
Like cherries in a summer light.
Coconuts tumble, oh what a sight,
I duck for cover, oh what a fright!

The sand is hot—my toes feel fried,
A beach ball rolls, I can't decide.
Catch it, kick it, don't let it stray,
Oops, there it goes, I'm starting to sway!

In this place where I lose my mind,
Funny stories leap, new friends to find.
So grab your hats, let's take a ride,
In heat-induced joy, we'll all abide!

Ripples in the Sultry Air

With every step, my shirt clings tight,
Like a bear hug gone a tad too light.
I'm a walking sponge, drenched and bold,
Looking like a snack but feeling old!

The ice cubes dance, they're feeling free,
While I stay stuck like a flavored pea.
A lizard grins, oh what a tease,
He moves so fast, I think he's on breeze!

Pineapple hats and shades so bright,
We're all swimming in the daylight.
Sweaty brows, oh, what a show,
As we shuffle on, nice and slow!

In sultry air, we find our sway,
With giggles loud to chase heat away.
Let's bask in laughter and feel the flair,
As we skip along, without a care!

The Warmth that Awakens

Awakened by heat, it hugs me tight,
As I rise up, the sun's a sight.
With breakfast pancakes stuck to my face,
I might just burst into a warm embrace!

Sipping coffee, oh what a thrill,
Like molten lava, it makes me ill.
A sip too hot, I jump and shout,
"Watch it! My mouth is in a drought!"

Flip-flops slap on the pavement hot,
I'm dancing to a beat, or just a lot.
With each step, I feel the burn,
Is it the sun, or my wild turn?

So let's embrace this funny plight,
And laugh and sweat from morn till night.
With warmth that wakes and leaves us bright,
Together we'll face the summer's light!

Fervent Whispers of the Breeze

The air is thick, oh what a tease,
Feeling sticky like warm cheese.
I chase a breeze, but where'd it go?
It left me sweating, moving slow.

The sun is shining with such zeal,
I see a mirage, or is it real?
My drink is melting by the hour,
Someone send me ice, I need that power!

A fan blows softly, my cool friend,
But only when it's near the end.
I leap around, a silly sight,
Trying to dance, oh what a fright!

With sunglasses perched upon my nose,
I'm feeling fabulous, I suppose.
The world is bright, the laughter free,
In sweltering joy, it's just you and me.

Dance of the Sunlit Shadows

The shadows stretch, they twist and prance,
I join right in, what a funny dance!
My feet are hot, is that a smoke?
Where's my ice pack? This ain't a joke!

The sun's a spotlight on my skin,
In this bright show, do I have to grin?
My hat's a shield, a floppy mess,
Waving at clouds, oh, where's the rest?

I tell the sun to take a break,
And strengthen my drink, for goodness' sake!
Every step's a comedy made,
In this blazing parade, I can't evade.

So here I stand, a shade of red,
A beach ball bouncing, oh, what a spread!
With laughter echoing all around,
We dance, we twist on this sunlit ground.

A Symphony of Sweat

A drip, a drop, oh how it flows,
My shirt is clinging, everyone knows.
A symphony of sweat takes flight,
Conducted by the heat so bright.

I stroll along, a slick ballet,
Dodging puddles, in disarray.
A sip of lemonade, now that's the key,
To this sticky, funny jubilee!

The birds are chirping tunes so sweet,
While I'm orchestrating my retreat.
Slips and slides, oh what a scene,
Making a splash, a summer queen!

But nothing dampens the high of fun,
In this sweaty, chaotic run.
With laughter ringing all around,
In this symphony, pure joy is found.

Vivid Nights Under Starlit Skies

As the sun dips low, the colors bloom,
I wave goodbye to the heat's hot room.
The stars come out to join the show,
While I try to cool down, but oh no!

The fireflies dance, a neon spree,
I stumble and laugh, just me and me.
With a jug of punch, I know the score,
Sipping slowly, then begging for more!

The fun never stops in this warm sway,
Beneath the stars, we laugh and play.
The laughter's loud, the mood is right,
As we bask in joy of this splendid night.

So here's to the warmth and the funny glows,
In vivid nights, anything goes.
With friends beside and dreams to chase,
Under the stars, we find our place.

A Symphony of Humidity

The air is thick, like a warm soup,
Sweaty eyebrows join the fun group.
My hair's a frizz, a wild affair,
As I dance with my shirt in mid-air.

Ice cream drips like a joyful mess,
While flip-flops squeak, oh what a stress!
Lemonade rivers flow down my chin,
In this heat, sweat and laughter win!

Neighbors peek out to shout and cheer,
As I pirouette on my front lawn here.
But when nature calls, I dash up quick,
The sweat's a river, oh what a trick!

Fans are spinning, they're working hard,
I'll open my fridge, it's my cool card.
With popsicles clinging like loyal pets,
In this muggy bliss, I have no regrets!

Mango Skins and Ocean Dreams

Slathered in sunscreen, I'm ready to play,
Mango skins stick to my fingers today.
Waves crash around, I take a big leap,
Oops! Just belly-flopped, now it's hard to breathe!

Seagulls squawk, they're stealing my fries,
While I sip coconut, full of surprise.
The juice runs down like a summer thrill,
In this sticky mess, I'm king of the grill!

I chase the shade, but it runs away,
Like my hopes of keeping the sun's rays at bay.
But laughter erupts, and fun's on the rise,
As we build sandcastles, it's winning my eyes!

Sticky fingers wave, a friendship so sweet,
Under the sun, life's a big treat.
With mango skins and joy in the seams,
Let's dance in the heat, pursue our wild dreams!

Radiance of the Overhead Sun

Sunshine's a trickster, making me bake,
My ice cream cone? An impossible stake!
With every drip, I chuckle and sigh,
As the sticky puddle winks goodbye.

Bikini contest? I'll skip the parade,
Instead, I'll find shade in a big leafy glade.
Cool drinks in hand, we share silly jokes,
The sun's laughing hard at these foolish folks!

Sizzling sidewalks, I hop like a hare,
Beware of the puddles that dare me to dare!
Flip-flops are squeaking, it's dance time, you see,
Under this sky, we're so wild and free!

The sun dips low, it's time to unwind,
With friends around, good vibes we find.
Radiating joy, in this bright fun run,
Here's to the laughter—our day's just begun!

Whispering Breezes of the Equator

The breeze dances in, oh what a tease,
Playing with hair, it brings me to my knees.
I wave at the heat, a playful embrace,
Chasing that wind with my happy face!

Coconut water spills on my shirt,
As I grin wide through the warmth and the dirt.
Colorful flip-flops splash on the ground,
As my dance with the sunshine only gets loud!

Sunglasses slip down my nose for a tease,
With every giggle, I'm begging for ease.
But come sunset, we'll toast in a line,
For the fun times ahead, oh they will be divine!

As stars twinkle and chase daylight away,
We'll laugh till we cry, come what may.
With whispers of warmth in the soft summer air,
We're free spirits, dancing without a care!

Swaying Palms in Scorching Sun

Under the palms, the children play,
While sweat beads form and drift away.
The ice cream melts, a sticky treat,
   As giggles echo in the heat.

Sandy toes and sunburned backs,
Our sunscreen's gone, we've lost the packs.
We laugh and moan as we can't see,
Who needs a bath? We're salt sea free!

The beach ball bounces in the sun,
With every throw, we shout and run.
A crab might join our playful mess,
   It pinches dad, oh what a stress!

As day turns night, the fireflies glow,
We roast some marshmallows, oh what a show!
With sticky fingers, we curl up tight,
Dream of the laughter, the sun's delight.

Mirage of the Distant Shore

A shimmering heat makes us all dream,
The waves look like they're hot chocolate cream.
We race to find the ocean's edge,
And trip on flip-flops, we pledge to hedge!

The horizon dances, it plays a trick,
Is that a whale or a big fat stick?
We wave to nothing and laugh so loud,
As seagulls circle like they're proud!

An umbrella flips—it's on a roll,
A little kid claims, 'Look! That's my pole!'
We search for shells, but find just chips,
Of snacks we've dropped during wild flips!

Yet strange treasures always abound,
Like sand in places all around.
We shake it off, with sandy glee,
At least we know we're wild and free!

Dance of the Sunlit Waves

The sun pops up with a fiery grin,
We dive in first—let summer begin!
The water's warm, the laughter's loud,
We splash like crazy, crazy crowd!

The jellyfish dance in a silly way,
With tentacles flapping, they join our play.
A beach ball bounces, a dog runs fast,
He steals our snacks—oh, what a blast!

The sun sits high, we're toast on bread,
But we don't care, we've puns instead!
A sunburned nose and hats askew,
Making memories, just me and you!

The tides roll in with a gentle sigh,
"More drinks!" we shout, as the day drifts by.
With tired limbs and hearts so light,
We wave farewell to another bright night.

Vibrance Under Fading Skies

As daylight fades, the stars appear,
We pop some corn that we brought near.
The sky's a canvas painted bold,
While giggles twist through the evening gold.

The sunset paints a ridiculous hue,
Like cotton candy, just for you.
We chase the crickets, their chirps a song,
While fireflies flicker, all night long!

A beach chair tips, a tumbler's fate,
The lemonade spills—oh, isn't that great?
As our voices rise in evening's cheer,
We toast to mishaps, let's give a cheer!

With blankets tossed and snacks all shared,
The warmth of friendship keeps us paired.
Under fading skies, the fun won't cease,
We'll laugh our way to nightly peace.

The Sultry Serenade of Summer

The sun is shining, oh so bright,
My ice cream's melting, what a sight!
Rooftop dancing, we lose our way,
Sweat and laughter blend in play.

Fans are spinning, woes take flight,
Comfy chairs turned into fright.
Summer flings us, we twirl around,
In this sauna, joy is found.

Cacti giggle, the flowers sway,
How to keep cool? That's the game play.
Jump in the kiddie pool, take a splash,
We're all just kids in a sun-blazed bash.

Sizzling skies with a side of fun,
Chasing shadows, we're on the run.
A popsicle stick, a laughter sound,
In this heat, pure joy's unbound.

Heat-Hazed Horizons in Paradise

Mirage dances in the street,
Hoses spraying, oh, what a treat!
Flip-flops squeaking on the ground,
Lost in laughter, we spin around.

Palm trees giggle, playing along,
Sipping coconut, feel so strong.
We're in the fryer, can't complain,
The sun's spun here, it's all a game!

Sunburned noses, bright as can be,
Slathered in sunscreen, sticky spree.
At the beach, we build our dreams,
In this heat, nothing's as it seems.

Seashells whisper, secrets fly,
Ice coffee melts, oh my, oh my!
Every wave brings a new surprise,
Under the sun, our spirits rise.

When Cicadas Sing Their Rhythms

Cicadas buzz a silly tune,
Croaking frogs join in, oh swoon!
Breezes tease, they tug my hair,
In this warmth, we've not a care.

Lemonade stands on every street,
Pour a cup and find your seat.
Kids run wild, with sticky hands,
Chasing dreams in summer lands.

Fireflies dance as the sun dips low,
We're in a dream, don't want to go.
Barefoot walking, feel that heat,
With each step, the world's a treat!

Silly hats and shades too big,
Sippin' cocktails, do a jig.
Laughter echoes, can't resist,
In this heat, joy, we insist!

Floating Dreams on Warm Winds

Kites are soaring, colors bright,
Warm winds carry a feathered flight.
Kids on scooters, summer's zest,
In this heat, we're all the best.

Tanning lotion, scents divine,
Bubbly drinks, we're feeling fine!
Picnic blankets, a shaded nook,
Fruity snacks, and storybooks.

Pineapple hats and banana shoes,
Laughter shared, we can't lose.
Dance in the waves, skip the rocks,
In this warmth, joy unlocks.

Days blur in this sunny maze,
Memories made in sunlit haze.
With sunshine smiles and hearts so free,
We're living life—just you and me!

Sunkissed Serenade

The sun's a prankster, oh so bright,
Playful rays tickle with delight.
Sunscreen's on, but I still fry,
Like bacon sizzled in the sky.

Laughter echoes with each step,
Ice cream melting, I must prep.
A dance of sweat down my back,
Who needs a sauna? Here's the hack!

Hats oversized, we strut and preen,
Fashion statements, pure sunscreen.
Flip-flops flapping, like we're mad,
This silly heat just makes us glad!

So raise a glass, let's toast this heat,
Who needs a cool breeze? We've got our feet!
In joyful chaos, we bask and grin,
Sun-kissed and wild, let the fun begin!

Dance of the Heat Haze

A shimmer wiggles on the ground,
The pavement's doing a funky round.
I step, I slip, it's quite the show,
Waltzing with shadows, to and fro.

The drapes are swaying, curtains tease,
Thermometers beg, "Oh, please!
Cool me down, I'm losing my mind!"
But who needs sanity? We're so unrefined!

My drink's a slush that lost its way,
Who knew ice could run off in dismay?
Giggling as I find my shade,
A human puddle in the parade.

So let us sway, X-rated heat,
Dance like we're brazen, feel the beat.
Laugh with abandon, let worries freeze,
In this blazing haze, we do as we please!

Tempestuous Tranquility

Sweat beads form a beaded crest,
In this sauna where we jest.
Fans are blowing, but it's no use,
I roast like toast, what's the excuse?

A hammock sways beneath the sun,
I nap while battling heat—who's won?
Flip-flops scatter, all in a mess,
This lazy dance, I must confess.

Birds are squawking, dogs just sigh,
Even the ants seem to comply.
I raise my drink, a frosty sight,
Cheers to this heat, our sweet plight!

So here we lounge, in sunlit bliss,
With laughter swirling, who could miss?
In this tempest, we find our peace,
In heat's embrace, our joy won't cease!

Sweltering Starlight

Stars peek out through thick, warm air,
As sunset blushes, without a care.
The moon's a joker, casting beams,
Of summer giggles and daydreams.

Fireflies blink in a balmy haze,
While I sweat through this endless daze.
The hammock's calling, oh what delight,
In this steamy, serene night!

Just as I settle, the crickets play,
They chirp a tune, come join the fray.
A burp from dinner, a giggle's release,
This laughter's magic, pure, without cease.

So let's embrace the sticky absurd,
In moonlit mischief, find joy unheard.
With a sigh and a grin, we'll dance till the morn,
In sweltering starlight, our spirits reborn!

The Radiance of Forgotten Shores

The sun's so bright, it's lost its mind,
My ice cream's melting, oh so unkind!
Flip-flops stuck, oh what a mess,
Seagulls laugh, my beachwear's a dress!

Sandy feet and coconut shade,
Dreaming of cool with a lemonade.
The fish say hello, then swim away,
I swear they mock me - it's not okay!

A crab in sunglasses strolls past me,
I think he knows summer's key!
Sunburnt faces, giggles galore,
The fun of heat, who could ask for more?

Forget the clouds, they're far too shy,
When it's hot enough to fry an egg, oh my!
Yet laughter dances with every wave,
In this sunlit chaos, we're all brave!

Poems Beneath the Palms

Underneath palms, the heat's absurd,
My thoughts become a jumbled herd.
Sweat rolls down like a silly stream,
Making me question if this is a dream!

Coconuts grin, giving me shade,
While I suppose I should be laid.
But no, I'm bouncing like a beach ball,
Chasing the breeze, I'm having a ball!

A parrot squawks, 'Just chill, my friend,'
But I can't stop, the fun won't end!
Sun hats flying like kites on high,
While flip-flops dance and make me sigh!

When shades are down, the laughter's loud,
In our little crew, we're all so proud.
We'll cast our worries far away,
In this sunny madness, let's play!

Heat's Lament in Time

The time is stuck in a molten pool,
My brain is fried; I feel like a fool.
As sizzles and pops become the song,
I doubt the sun even knows right from wrong!

Ice cubes melt faster than my stride,
Chasing them down, I feel the slide.
The air is thick like a stew today,
With giggles escaping, come what may!

My beach towel won, it hugs the sand,
As I attempt a sunbathed stand.
Sweaty socks snicker, I can't let go,
What a fine play in the heat's grand show!

So here I stand, a pickle in bliss,
Wishing for an ice bath with a kiss.
But for now, I'll laugh, I'll dance, I'll sway,
In this warm embrace, I'll play all day!

Where the Warm Breezes Roam

Where the warm breezes twist and twirl,
I tumble and spin, ready to whirl.
The sun does its dance, a shiny ghost,
While pineapples wear sunglasses, oh my, most!

Dripping with jokes and endless cheer,
I chase a piña colada – come here!
But seagulls snatch it with glee in their eyes,
In this zany land, I'm full of surprise!

Sandy castles attempt to stand tall,
While the tide giggles and shouts, "You'll fall!"
Me, falling into laughter, oh what a sight,
In this sizzling world, everything feels right!

So let's raise a toast to the sunshine bold,
With laughs like sunshine, together we hold.
In the realm of warm breezes, we'll roam free,
In this heat we'll find our harmony!

A Sonnet of the Sultry Sea

The sun beams down, a frying pan's delight,
I thought I'd swim, but even fish took flight.
Sunscreen thick, like frosting on a cake,
If I stay still, will I start to bake?

With every step, the pavement's like a grill,
I dance a jig to keep my toes from frill.
The seagulls squawk as if they've lost their minds,
Trying to find a shade that's hard to find.

The waves invite with promises of cool,
Yet even mermaids hide from sun at school.
I swap my beach ball for a sprinkler hose,
My sunburn grins, the only friend that grows.

Each summer day feels like a bad joke's sting,
In the land where even lizards start to sing.

Vibrance Beneath the Canopy

Coconuts drop like drums from the trees,
I dance with monkeys, sharing light breeze.
The shade's a treasure, a pirate's delight,
While ants march by, in their tiny plight.

Sweaty brows glisten, a shiny parade,
Finding cold drinks—oh the prices they wade!
The hammock swings, I'm almost in flight,
Til a frog lands near, who gives me a fright.

Vines creep around like a child in a game,
I hide from the sun, though it found me the same.
Did I just see a toucan with style?
Maybe it's time for a tropical smile?

The laughter echoes, a melody sweet,
In this vibrant jungle, life can't be beat.

Nightfall Caress of Heat

As daylight fades to a sultry kiss,
The fireflies blink, I can't help but miss.
The evening whispers, "Cool down, my friend,"
But my ice cream's melting—will summer end?

Soda cans pop like fireworks above,
While the stars look down, the night's in love.
I sit on the porch, feeling quite grim,
Yet the neighbor's cat? It's a bolting whim!

With fans failing, I'm a puddle of me,
The heat's a villain, plotting with glee.
My best idea is to dance on the mat,
Who knew my moves would scare off the cat?

So here I remain, in the warmth of delight,
Wishing for breezes, but finding good nights.

Embracing the Golden Glare

Sunflowers stand like sentinels bright,
A golden glare, oh what a sight.
With hats too big, and shades that clash,
I step outside, in a sweat-soaked splash.

The ice cream truck plays its jolly tune,
And chasing it feels like a funny cartoon.
But melting cones bring a sticky plight,
As a bee buzzes in for a sugary bite.

Beach towels stretched like blankets on sand,
A parade of flip-flops, a flip and a stand.
But one faux pas, a slip and a fall,
I'm now a sandcastle, quite proud at all!

So here's to the sun, with its laughter so bright,
In this golden embrace, we'll dance through the night.

Living in the Radiant Moment

Under the sun, I start to sweat,
My ice cream's melting, what a threat!
The pavement's sizzling, birds wear hats,
While I stuff my face with rinds of fat.

Palm trees wiggle, trying to cool,
Swaying like dancers, oh what a fool!
Flip-flops squeak, they join in the fun,
As I chase my shadow, I've nowhere to run.

Sunblock's my armor, white as a ghost,
Yet every flip turns me into toast.
With each step, I make a splash,
Waves of laughter, can't help but crash.

So here I bask, in sunlit delight,
Living it up in the glorious light.
With every giggle, each silly dance,
In this radiant moment, I take my chance!

Sunkissed Hues of Longing

I dream of beaches while stuck in a line,
My drink's too warm; can I borrow yours, wine?
Ice cubes melt faster than I can think,
Every sip's a shadow of frosty pink.

I wear shades indoors; I'm a fashion king,
Trying to look cool but my molecules sing.
The heat is a jester, playing tricks on my mind,
Laughing as I wipe sweat, oh so unkind!

Flip-flops and shorts, it's my summer attire,
Yet all I can think of is cooler desire.
When a breeze finally hovers, I start to swoon,
Wishing for winter, howling at the moon.

But with every chuckle, my heart grows bold,
These sunkissed hues turn my worries to gold.
So here's to the laughter, the joy that we find,
In sweet sunshine moments, we leave doubts behind!

Essence of Elation

Warm winds tickle under spinning fans,
My hair's a mess, let's all make plans!
A dance with the ice cubes is what I'll do,
Join them in chaos, who knew they could brew?

Sun hats and giggles, blending like paint,
Strutting around like I'm someone quaint.
Grilled hot dogs thrill while seagulls dive,
I'm just a snack in this sun-kissed hive.

Friendships sizzling, laughter that's grand,
We're all just kids, with sunshine so planned.
Doing the limbo, trying not to fall,
In this essence of joy, let's dance with all!

And when the day fades, we'll reminisce,
Of inflatable flamingos and summer bliss.
In our quirky moments, we truly see,
The funny little things, wild and carefree!

The Lingering Kiss of Light

The sun peeks in, an uninvited guest,
Rays bouncing around, giving cheeks a zest.
Bikini tops tangled, oh what a sight,
Trying to swim, but I'm stuck in the light!

Lemonade stands have gone to my head,
I dance on the grass, no worries or dread.
Life's a party with laughter and cheer,
With every warm glow, my worries disappear.

Flip-flops are flying, as we race down the street,
With every step, I can feel the beat.
The twilight calls, it's twilight's tease,
As we chase fireflies, shoulder to knees.

Here in this wonder, where time stands still,
The lingering kiss of light gives a thrill.
Let's soak in the moments, and giggle with glee,
For this dance with sunshine is where we're meant to be!

The Palette of Summer Nights

The sun dips low with a golden grace,
Ice cream drips down a laughing face.
Fans spin fast like a merry-go-round,
In this balmy circus, joy can be found.

Lemons dance in a pitcher so bright,
Cicadas chirp, oh what a delight!
Bare feet sizzling on pavement's embrace,
We toast to summer with frosty grace.

Neighbors argue over the best grill,
While kids play tag, giving us a thrill.
Fireflies twinkle like stars on the run,
As laughter echoes—'Can we get more sun?'

Flip-flops flapping, we chase the ice truck,
Each frozen treat feels like pure luck.
Sunglasses worn at the beach like a crown,
In this palette, we never frown.

Visions in the Heat

Sweat beads form like tiny jewels,
While we splash in imaginary pools.
Lemonade stands pop up like weeds,
As laughter bubbles from playful deeds.

The sun's a comedian, burning us right,
We wear t-shirts but forget them at night.
The grill's like a dragon, puffing out smoke,
Hot dogs sizzle, it's a gourmet joke.

Bright umbrellas blossom along the sand,
We dig for treasure—oh, isn't it grand?
A crab in sunglasses strolls by with flair,
While seagulls plot our picnic affair.

Sipping spritzers, we toast and we cheer,
Each gulp a giggle, the fun's in the air.
As the horizon melts into shades of red,
We dance under stars, laughing instead.

Blazing Footprints on the Shore

Footprints sizzle in the midday glow,
Flip-flops abandon me; on I go!
Seagulls squawk out the latest gossip,
While children make sandcastles, never stop.

The waves bring whispers, 'Dive in, just try!'
While coolers are stocked with drinks to supply.
Sunburned noses and all-over tan lines,
This beach day charms, sparking crazy designs.

A beach ball bounces, escaping the crew,
Someone trips over a towel, oh what a view!
The sun-cream fiasco, a slippery slide,
With sunscreen battles for laughter and pride.

As twilight arrives, the bonfire glows,
We roast marshmallows, see how it goes.
With every giggle, the night feels so fine,
In this blazing chaos, we truly shine.

Whispers of the Warm Winds

Warm winds come whispering secrets so bold,
They play with our hair, wonders unfold.
Chasing our dreams like a kite in the sky,
We giggle and stumble, oh my, oh my!

Balloons float high, like wishes untold,
As shade becomes nectar, pure and gold.
Sipping cold drinks while lounging in style,
As the world slows down, we sway for a while.

Friends make a ruckus with playful debate,
Over who caught the biggest fish—oh, it's fate!
But rumors are swirling in the hot summer air,
That the fish told tales of a giant's rare flair.

With laughter echoing against the warm tide,
We dance to the rhythm, hearts open wide.
As the sun dips low, we toss back our heads,
Whispering secrets, 'Let's party instead!'

Sand and Sea in Harmony

On the beach, I lost my shoe,
But found a crab who waved, it's true.
They form a band in sandy haze,
With ocean beats, we dance and play.

Seagulls squawk, they tease and jest,
While sunscreen drips from every vest.
A beach ball lands right on my face,
Giggles echo in this wild place.

My ice cream melts in the sun's embrace,
As sand sticks to me, what a race!
But laughing waves splash the shore,
In this festive scene, who could ask for more?

From sunburnt knees to sandy toes,
We roll and tumble, that's how it goes.
In harmony with the sun and sea,
A perfect day, just crab and me.

A Lament for the Liquid Sun

Oh, liquid sun, you've melted me,
I tried to dance, but now I flee.
My ice coffee turned to a puddle,
While on the pavement, I start to muddle.

Each drop of sweat's a minute lost,
Yet lemonade's worth any cost.
My brain is fried, yet I still grin,
In this hot mess, I'll just dive in.

I wear my hat like a big umbrella,
It flaps and waves, quite the fella!
I chase my thoughts like I chase a breeze,
But all I catch are swarming bees.

So raise a glass, let's toast the day,
To sticky limbs in sun's bright sway.
Though I may whine, I won't despair,
For laughter blooms in heat and glare.

Feast of the Summer Solstice

At noon, the burgers sizzle loud,
With smoke that's sure to draw a crowd.
A feast laid out beneath the sun,
Where every dish is overdone.

The grill's a sizzling artist's stage,
With fire that could ignite a page.
In flip-flops, we two-step around,
While drinks get shaken, not just found.

My friend brings out a giant pie,
But underheat, it starts to cry.
A watermelon, now rather deformed,
Becomes a punchline that's quite the norm.

Yet sunburned noses share the jokes,
In laughter, we're all happy folks.
A solstice feast can't go amiss,
Heat or not, it's pure bliss.

The Scorching Muse

The sun's my muse, or so I claim,
But rather it's a fiery game.
Writing poems in sweat-slicked sheets,
As ants parade around my feet.

I find the shade, oh sweet relief,
Yet nature teases, that's my grief.
A breeze arrives, but it won't stay,
Only flutters dust my way.

Inspiration comes, but I just flop,
As ice cubes melt, we're on the hop.
What wise words come in heated bliss?
A daffy rhyme, it can't be amiss.

So here I sit, with thoughts askew,
In this heat, I chuckle too.
The scorching muse, I'll never fight,
For laughter thrives in blinding light.

Seasons of the Scorching Sun

On beach chairs we sit, like pancakes too fried,
With sunscreen so thick, we slip on our slide.
The ice cream melts fast, a drippy mess spree,
We laugh at our fate, like critters on spree.

The ocean's a tease, it's warm as a bath,
A seagull swoops down, oh what a cool wrath!
The flip-flops are stuck, my foot's in a funk,
While sand's creeping in, like a mischievous skunk.

The beach ball rolls on, under bright glaring rays,
We chase it in circles, in silly sun haze.
It's hot as a sauna, but smiles keep us free,
We dance to the waves, wild and carefree.

As dusk brings a breeze, oh chill in the air,
We gather to share tales, with laughter to spare.
With hearts feeling light, and spirits like kites,
We wave to the sun, as it fades into nights.

Craze of the Raging Light

The sun peeks around with a grin so absurd,
Like pranks on the beach, it's utterly stirred.
We stumble on waves, like jellyfish sprawl,
While hair flies around, in a light-hearted brawl.

Palm trees are dancing, with hats on their leaves,
They sway in delight, while the funny sun cleaves.
Each sip of lemonade is a sweet joyful blast,
While ants do the cha-cha, with rhythm so fast.

Shady spots become jewels, where we gather our loot,
With snacks fitting for kings and hats looking cute.
We trade all our glasses for shades of bright glee,
While sunburns make us look like lobsters set free.

As night makes its move, the stars start to wink,
With laughter and snacks, we pop open a drink.
In the glow of the moon, we celebrate this plight,
At the craze of the day, and the charm of the night.

Echoes of the Glimmering Gulf

The gulf shimmers bright, like glitter on skin,
With splashes and giggles, let the fun times begin.
Floppy hats flying, on heads with no care,
As laughter erupts like it's floating in air.

The seagulls join in, with squawks full of sass,
They dive for our snacks, just like merry little brats.
Sandcastles crumble, under giggles galore,
While sunscreen's like glue, but we still want more.

Barefoot in chaos, with each silly slip,
We tumble and roll, with laughter we grip.
Ice-cream drips down, like a colorful trail,
While jellyfish waltz to a balmy sea tale.

As we gather 'round, for the sunset parade,
With stories of joy, in the light and the shade.
So here's to the echoes, of fun all day long,
In the glimmering gulf, where we all feel so strong.

Scents of the Sun-Baked Earth

The ground's hot enough to bake a pizza pie,
With sunflowers nodding, and clouds wandering by.
The grass sings a tune, as we jump with delight,
While the bugs join the party, in their tiny flight.

Watermelons glowing, like gems from the farm,
A juicy explosion, oh that's quite the charm!
We snack under trees, with laughter that spreads,
While ants hold a conference, on crumbs from our spreads.

Sun hats all tangled, like hair in a fight,
With friends in high spirits, our worries take flight.
Oh, the joys of the sun, with hugs and with smiles,
We play silly games, and forget all our trials.

As evening comes near, the stars take their place,
We gather together, with love to embrace.
With scents of the earth, where laughter won't cease,
We celebrate life, in silly, warm peace.

www.ingramcontent.com/pod-product-compliance
Lightning Source LLC
Chambersburg PA
CBHW072218070526
44585CB00015B/1396